Trigger Warning:
Self-Harm
Loss
Death
Suicide
Physical Abuse
Sexual Abuse

This book talks about my personal struggle with these topics, if you have or are currently struggling with these topics- this book may not be for you.
Thank you.
- J. DAL

Special Mentions:
To my siblings- For so long I wanted to be a good example for you. I wanted to show you that it was possible to follow your dreams and that you didn't have to wait for the "right time" let this book be the example, the time will be right when you make it right. I love you.

To my mother- I have wanted nothing more in my lifetime than for you to be proud of me, I hope this accomplishment is everything you dreamed for me and more. This is everything ive ever wanted and I know I was able to accomplish it because you were always there to push me, most of my reading and writing interests come from you, in so many ways this book is a result of your inspiration. I love you.

To my father- I wish you could have been here to see my dreams come true. I hope I have made you proud. I love and miss you and I hope this shows you how true that stamen is. Fly High.

To Stacey, LC, and Stef- This book is as much mine as it is yours. I hope it lives up to your expectations. Know that you are holding a copy because you encouraged me to not hold myself back. This is for you. I love you.

To Jenna- I did it! Thank you for loving me all this time, I hope you enjoy it! I love you to the moon and back.

To TBD- This is how I say I'm sorry.

i. Abused

When you are young and you fantasize about the first time a man touches you,
you never picture lumps or bruises.
You picture a soft kiss and tenderness that bleeds into the morning,
Well, the bleeding was there but never a kiss.
No, he traded that virtue for my face and his fist.
You picture getting dressed up and going out and playing in the tide
but going out now only requires makeup so you can hide-
the cuts, the bumps, the long angry nights spent curled in a corner avoiding the fights. But you stay with him anyway because you still believe in the Fantasy
but sweet young girl the man you dreamed of
wouldn't't have done this.
would he?
-NAW

Ive learned to blend in. If I can be what you want me
to be. Then maybe you'll always want me…

-Chamaeleon

It's always two steps forward and three steps back,
I feel like Dorothy without a golden track.
And instead of ruby red slippers,
I have ruby red scars and scissors.
I never knew that somewhere over the rainbow
meant I'd have to deal with rain.
Though, I guess, i never was much of a Dorothy
but always the wicked witch of the west.

Truth is we don't "fall in love" we crawl, slide, scrape,
bleed, and limp our way into it.

-hope less, romantic.

Mirrors don't reflect anything but horrors.

-big girl in the reflection

Shakespeare had it right when he said "never was there a story of more woe than that of Juliet and her premature obsession with some guy named Romeo" or something like that.

-falls too quickly

If I'm being honest with myself, I think I get tattoos because even when I'm undressed, I'll be covered.

-body shamming

It is a slippery slope back into the black pit. And once you're in it, you're stuck there in its tar, until it surrounds you and becomes familiar again.
-depression

When did oxygen start burning when you need to breath?
-don't make him angry

I spend most of my days with my nose between the pages of someone else's life because I genuinely wish I could stop living mine.
I don't want to talk about it. If I talk about it I will surely be the reason that sank the little boat. And I loved that little Navy Boat.
-Mothership

I'm still waiting for the day when the memory of you is not followed by a gut-wrenching ache in the pit of my hallowed chest.
-grief

You know how when you go under water and the world finally goes quiet?
That's what it is like in my mind, dead silent.
But when you're lungs begin to burn for air in your mind
you can't push out of the water and make everything fine.
So you panic and the quiet becomes deadly,
the sound of silence becoming a part of your funeral medley

I nailed the pain of losing you on my heart with a hammer.
-miss you dad

No tattoo could carve you deep enough so I tried to myself… that's when I realized that my love was skin deep and yours never existed…
-NAW

Memories are funny things.
They are like dreams that came true…
Or nightmares you couldn't't wake up from…
Yeah, Memories are funny things.

Maybe I'm screaming at a pitch only my dog can hear
because he seems to be the only one who has noticed
that I'm struggle to breath over here.

Not all monsters hide under your bed.
No, most monsters I have met
Reside inside my head.
-depression and anxiety
The Civil War has nothing
On the blood ive shed
While fighting the battle
In my mind.
-blood-stained arms.

I must be a bull
Because all the red flags
Seem to attract me.
-used and abused

Some games are not meant for children
And you should have never played with me.
I can not remember your face but I remember
Your voice as it commented on how I taste.
You said the game would be fun,
But I remember wanting it to end in haste.
Some games are not meant for children
And you should have never played with me.

I don't remember my first time
Because he decided it was better
For me to not be awake and
I decided to trust whatever
Drink he made.
-I was only 14 NAW

Sometimes I wonder if my
Razor blades ever get
Jealous of my tattoos.
-trigger warning

I miss the tingling feeling of your
Fingertips against my palms,
A gentle reminder that
you were right there.
Now all I have is a numbness in my
Heart that reminds that you are gone.

-Rest in Peace, Dad.

Dating seems like a lot more fun in the movies.
Must come naturally when someone writes
A script that includes a "happy ending"
Before you ever get there.
Yet, somehow, I deserve an Oscar for the
Dating scenes, I've improved over the years.

You know the part in movies,
When someone is dying
And everything starts to move in
Slow motion and you can literally
Feel the main character's heartbeat?
It is real.
-Rest in Peace, Dad.

Fire and Gasoline must
Fume with jealousy at how
Destructive we are for each other.
-NAW

I wish I could be the daughter you
Want and not the daughter you got
Stuck with.
-I just want to make you proud.

I promise to stop promising things I know I can not
honor.
-liar.

Loving you was as easy as breathing
And as suffocating as being buried alive.
-NAW

ii. Awakening

Even as I'm typing this, I know I will never press send.
You see somethings are better left unsaid.
What do words matter anyway?
Nothing I say can take away the sting of your pain.
And even as tears fell from my eyes like rain,
My lies raged on like a fire caught on trees,
and Unlike bumblebees, who are gentle and produce sweet honey,
my tongue is more like a wasp,
and something that destructive thinks casualties are funny.
But the jokes on me cause now your gone and I'm left cold and hungry-
for your voice and your ocean blue eyes.
I remember a time where I wanted to drown in them
and now I'm drowning in goodbyes.
Sometimes an old song will come on and I imagine us dancing around
and then I trip over my own feet because I realize that I am bound,
grief and guilt gag me like as if to punish me for the past.
I take it willingly because I know now that I am strong enough now to last.
And if I said I'm sorry tonight and hit send, and beg for forgiveness,
Please tell me, what would you say then?
Would it be a sweet reunion like the honey from the bees?
Or would you tie the noose and hang me from the burning trees?

-TBD

Sometimes I pretend I'm still eleven and waiting for my Hogwarts Acceptance letter because the reality that I'm a 23 year old, single waitress seems less magical.
-would have been a Gryffindor

When you see me I want you to actually see me.
Stop looking through me.
I'm right here.
This is me.
Do you even want to see me?
Or do you just want to see my green?
-CDP

Tirelessly resting in stages that are nuclear.

-TBD

I'm not sure what the worst thing that happened to me is…
but I was certain you were the best thing the moment I memorized
the sound of your voice when you said my name.
I wished I could download it to the sound of my heartbeat,
and put in on replay when it would rain outside, and the world became heavy.
You see I could never carry the weight of this world but I could always carry the weight of that memory,
you and me in the back seat of your chevy- tangled in our perfect melody.
-My Country Boy.

He is not him, but he makes the pain go away. He is a warm hug to lean into at the end of the day. He is a gentle breeze that whispers between the trees. He is easy. He is kind… but he is not the one that once was mine.

-CP

Sometimes I wonder if he remembers the sound of my breathing the way he remembers the memory of me bleeding…
-TBD

.
Sometimes I wonder if I should ask you flat out ask
you if want my bank information instead of you
pretending like having me around because you love
me was your only motivation.
-CDP

When I pictured my safe place,
I used to picture an ocean view. However, when I
found my safe place
it was here with you.
An oceans length of love and deep conversation,
ended up being my strangest salvation.

-SLCS

I've lived a thousand different lives in the comfort of my bed covers with a reading light.
- Coping skills

I have discovered more about myself in the words of someone else's story than I have while writing my own.
-am I even an author?

If it is true that love runs as deep and wide as the ocean,
It would explain why your eyes are so blue.
-TBD

I scream "I love you" just for you to whisper back "I
like spending time with you"
-My Country Boy

Why is it when I find something I love to do that is
different
Then something you would have chosen; you label it
weird?
Can you not just celebrate that I found something
that make me
Feel like myself? Or is it simply that you never
wanted me to find
Who I am but remain in the shadow of who you never
were?

-yeah, I make tik toks.

Thought of you constantly run through my mind,
And I hope that, at the very least, I sometimes
Walk through yours.
-TBD

He is not him.
But he makes the pain go away.
He is a warm hug
To lean into at the end of the day.
He is a gentle breeze
That whispers off the sea.
He is easy.
He is kind.
But he is not the one I once called "mine".
-CDP

iii.   Ascending

Dear Future Husband,
There are some things you should know about me. First, I am damaged. I will struggle to trust you and that is not your fault. You see, past relationships have taught me that love comes with consequences, and I tend to want to shelter the people I love from the consequences that come from loving me. Second, I will try and convince you that I am not good enough for you. Not because I am not good enough but because I don't believe that I am. I have never felt good enough, more than that I have never felt like enough. For anyone. Including myself. Third, I give up on myself a lot, but I will never give up on you. Ask anyone who knows about how much I will defend someone I love. Ask them about my loyalty to those people who I'm sure they believe did not deserve my loyalty. I am loyal to a fault and that is something about myself that I do love. Everyone deserves someone who will love them with that kind of passion. And I am sure that, whoever you are, you will be the source of that passion that burns within me. And lastly, my love, if I have made it long enough to find you… then i am stronger than I ever pictured I was when I wrote this and if that the case, you will be marrying one of the fiercest versions of myself that ever existed, and for your sake- I pray you can handle it. Cause even now, my strength amazes me. Until we say our vows to one another, I vow to grow and learn to use that fire and passion that burns inside of me to burn bridges with my insecurities and light my way through those dark places until I find you.

Always yours,
Your Future Wife.

I did it broken.
I did it scared.
I did it crying.
I did it without you.
I'm still doing it.

When it comes to my girls,
I find strength in their victories.
And clarity in their journeys.
-SLCSJ

I have found that there is magic at the joint of a pen
and paper.
-healing.

Healing is a lot like the events at Jericho, my walls
must simply come down.
-Christian woman

Healing is a lot like grief in the sense that
It comes in waves.

We are like the rough rocks that litter the
Shore and over time
As the tides of change steadily come
In and out,
It begins to wear down our sharp edges,
Cracks, dents, and all the things
We consider about ourselves to be
"broken" until we are new smooth stones.

Healing often looks like grieving all over again.
- It takes time.

Healing unlocks worlds you never knew existed.
-a whole new world.

Have you ever considered,
as the reader, that you have
unfiltered access to my,
the writers, most inner thoughts?
-This feels vulnerable.

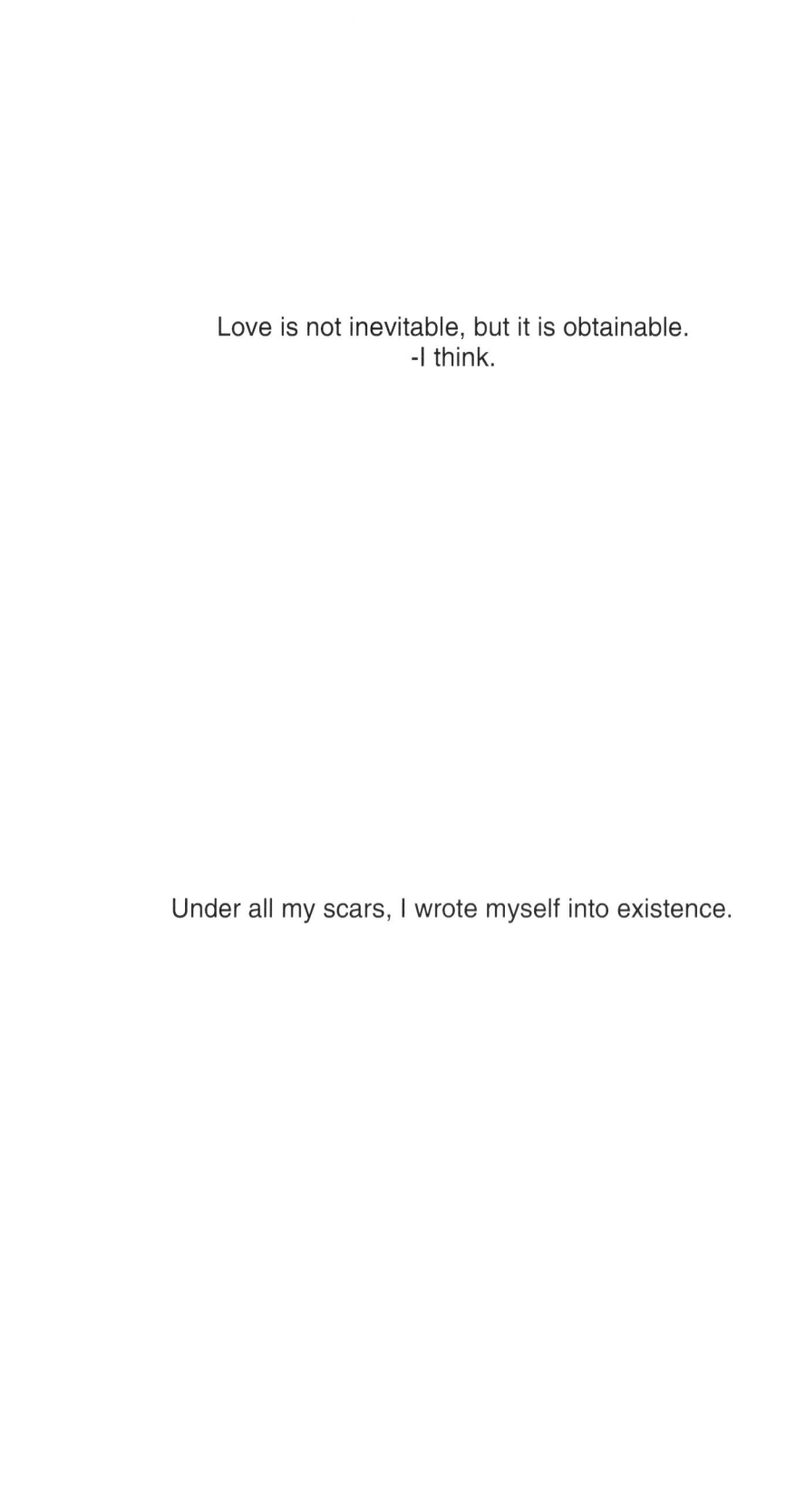

Love is not inevitable, but it is obtainable.
-I think.

Under all my scars, I wrote myself into existence.

Made in the USA
Middletown, DE
20 September 2021